THE AMAZING HUMAN BODY

THE HUMAN
RESPIRATORY SYSTEM

by Tammy Gagne

BrightPoint Press

San Diego, CA

BrightPoint Press

© 2025 BrightPoint Press
an imprint of ReferencePoint Press, Inc.
Printed in the United States

For more information, contact:
BrightPoint Press
PO Box 27779
San Diego, CA 92198
www.BrightPointPress.com

ALL RIGHTS RESERVED.

No part of this work covered by the copyright hereon may be reproduced or used in any form or by any means—graphic, electronic, or mechanical, including photocopying, recording, taping, web distribution, or information storage retrieval systems—without the written permission of the publisher.

LIBRARY OF CONGRESS CATALOGING-IN-PUBLICATION DATA

Name: Gagne, Tammy, author.
Title: The human respiratory system / by Tammy Gagne.
Description: San Diego, CA: BrightPoint Press, 2025 | Series: The amazing human body | Audience: Grade 7 to 9 | Includes bibliographical references and index.
Identifiers: ISBN: 9781678209643 (hardcover) | ISBN: 9781678209650 (eBook)
The complete Library of Congress record is available at www.loc.gov.

CONTENTS

AT A GLANCE	4
INTRODUCTION HELPING PEOPLE BREATHE	6
CHAPTER ONE WHAT IS THE RESPIRATORY SYSTEM?	12
CHAPTER TWO HOW DOES THE RESPIRATORY SYSTEM WORK?	22
CHAPTER THREE WHAT CAN GO WRONG WITH THE RESPIRATORY SYSTEM?	32
CHAPTER FOUR WHAT CAN HUMANS DO TO KEEP THE RESPIRATORY SYSTEM HEALTHY?	46
Glossary	58
Source Notes	59
For Further Research	60
Index	62
Image Credits	63
About the Author	64

AT A GLANCE

- The human respiratory system takes oxygen into the body.

- All processes in the human body require oxygen. People need oxygen to digest food, move, and think.

- People breathe air into the body through the nose and the mouth. A tube called the trachea then carries the air to the lungs.

- Oxygen enters the bloodstream in the lungs. Blood then carries oxygen throughout the body.

- A waste gas called carbon dioxide leaves the body when a person breathes out.

- Illnesses can affect the human respiratory system. These illnesses include asthma, influenza, and lung cancer.

- Suffocation occurs when a person cannot get oxygen. This can happen due to choking, drowning, and other situations that restrict breathing.

- One of the best ways to keep the respiratory system healthy is by not smoking. Other ways include eating a healthy diet and exercising regularly.

INTRODUCTION

HELPING PEOPLE BREATHE

Su May Liew had a breathing problem as a child. Her chest sometimes made an odd sound. "I remember wheezing away, my chest going 'heee, heee,' like I was blowing a whistle," she said.[1] The sound worried her parents. They took her to a doctor.

The doctor told Liew that she had asthma. This condition causes a person's airways to swell. Asthma can make it hard

Doctors listen to patients' breathing to check for unusual sounds by using a tool called a stethoscope.

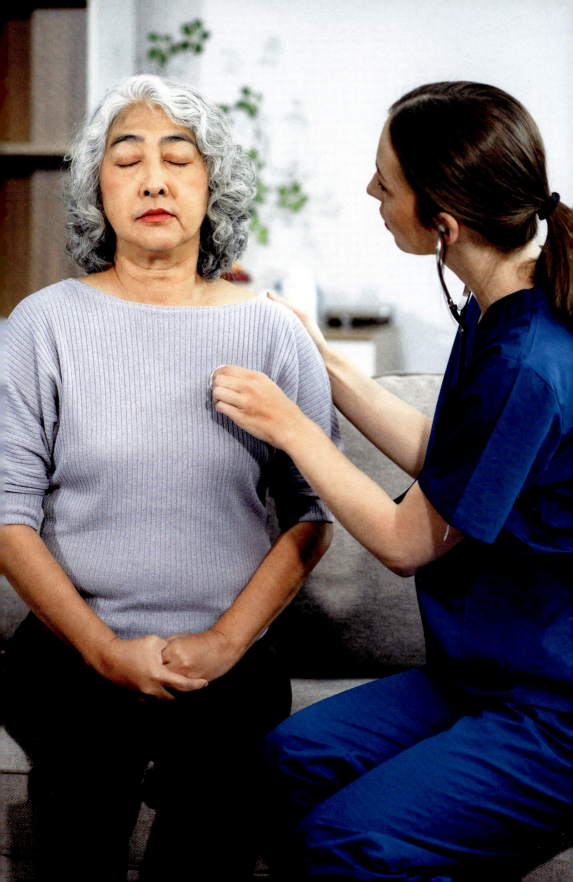

A metered dose inhaler is one type of inhaler. It pushes a puff of medicine into the user's mouth when the user presses the top of the device.

for a person to get enough air. Liew's doctor gave her pills to take when she wheezed. These pills relaxed her airways. This made it easier for her to breathe.

Liew became a doctor when she grew up. She decided to study breathing diseases. These include asthma. Treatments for asthma had improved since she was a child. Back then, doctors simply tried to stop asthma attacks when they happened. But Liew could give her patients medicine that prevented attacks. She was also able to deliver the medicine in better ways. Patients no longer needed to take pills. They could use inhalers instead. These devices allow people to breathe medicine into their lungs.

Liew was thankful that treatments for asthma had improved. Her young patients reminded her of her own childhood struggle with asthma. She was happy to make a difference in the lives of people with this respiratory condition.

The lungs are the main organs of the respiratory system.

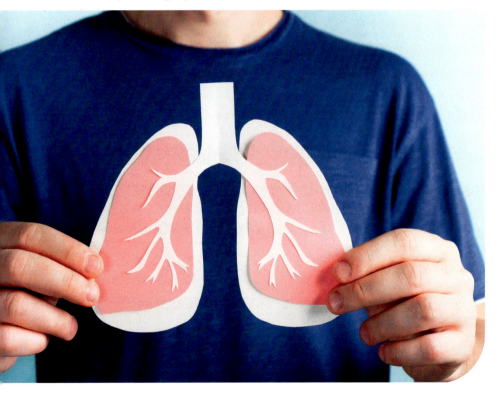

RESPIRATORY SYSTEM BASICS

The respiratory system is a group of organs in the human body. These organs make breathing possible. They take oxygen out of the air. Blood then carries oxygen throughout the body. Humans use this valuable substance to grow and function.

The respiratory system does other important jobs, too. For example, it allows people to smell and talk. Other body systems work with the respiratory system. Together, these systems make digestion, thinking, and movement possible.

CHAPTER ONE

WHAT IS THE RESPIRATORY SYSTEM?

The human respiratory system is always working. The average person takes about 25,000 breaths every day. "We pay no attention to this continuous activity as we work, play, and sleep," says Dr. Shawn Nishi.[2] But breathing is necessary for human life. People rely on the respiratory system to bring oxygen into their bodies. They also use it to release waste gases.

The average person breathes in about 2,000 gallons (7,600 L) of air per day.

Much of the body's oxygen is contained in water, which is made up of oxygen and hydrogen.

Air contains many gases. Nitrogen and oxygen make up about 99 percent of air. The remaining 1 percent comprises small amounts of many other gases. About 78 percent of air is nitrogen. Oxygen makes up about 21 percent of air. People breathe to get this element.

Oxygen is the most common element in the human body. It makes up about 65 percent of a person's mass. Almost all processes in the body require oxygen. For example, people need it to move. This is because muscles need oxygen to work. The more that people move, the more oxygen they need.

The creation of cells also requires oxygen. Cells are the basic units of living things. About 50 billion cells in a person's body die each day. The body uses oxygen to make new cells.

PART OF A BIGGER PICTURE

The respiratory system works closely with the body's circulatory system. This system includes the heart, blood vessels,

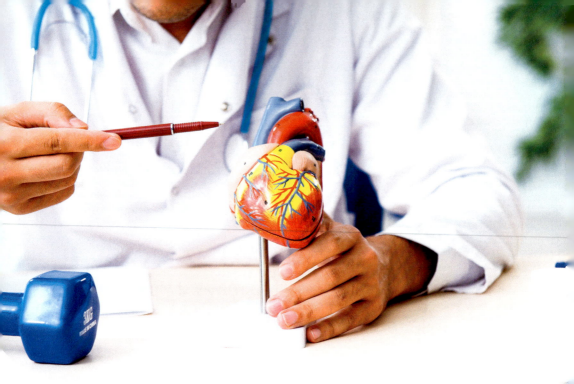

The average person's heart beats about 100,000 times every day.

and blood. Breathing brings oxygen into the blood. The heart then pumps the blood throughout the body. Blood carries oxygen to organs and other body tissues.

Breathing also removes waste gases from the body. Cells throughout the body use oxygen to make energy. This also produces carbon dioxide. The body releases this waste gas when a person breathes out.

The body must remove carbon dioxide to make space for oxygen. This is part of why people breathe heavily when exercising. Carbon dioxide can cause problems when it builds up in the blood. These problems include shortness of breath. Serious cases can cause seizures and a confused mental state.

Yawning

Yawning is a process of the respiratory system. A yawn begins with a large breath of air. It ends with exhalation. Scientists do not agree on exactly why people yawn. They think it serves many purposes. One is to increase alertness.

Breathing makes it possible for people to smell and speak. Smelling happens when a person breathes through their nose. Particles in the air travel to nerve cells high inside the nose. These cells then send messages to the brain. The brain reads these messages as a particular scent. Smell plays a big role in how food tastes. It can also warn people of nearby danger. For example, people can smell fire and rotting food.

Humans would not be able to talk without the respiratory system. People make sounds by exhaling air over their vocal cords. These cords rest in a part of the throat called the larynx. People can control their vocal cords. This allows them to change the pitch of their voice. The sound

The vocal cords produce different pitches by vibrating at different speeds. This allows people to hit a variety of notes when singing.

travels up the throat and into the nose and mouth. There, people further change the sound. They do this by moving their tongue and lips. This process allows people to make a wide range of sounds.

FILTERING THE AIR

People can inhale air through both the nose and mouth. The two openings of the nose are called nostrils. Air warms as it enters the nostrils. This happens as the air passes over warm blood vessels. This helps maintain the body's temperature. The nose contains tiny hairs called cilia. They trap dust and other small substances. These things could harm the body.

When people are ill, they may produce more mucus. This helps the body deal with the disease.

Mucus also helps trap substances that enter the body through the respiratory system. Mucus is a slippery fluid produced in many parts of the body. It is mostly made of water. Mucus also contains proteins and sugars. Special substances that fight germs are in mucus as well. Mucus keeps parts inside the body moist. This prevents these parts from getting irritated. For example, mucus helps food pass smoothly through the body.

CHAPTER TWO

HOW DOES THE RESPIRATORY SYSTEM WORK?

The respiratory system contains an upper airway and a lower airway. The upper airway is made up of the nose, **sinuses**, and throat. The mouth is also part of the upper airway.

The first step in breathing involves a large muscle called the diaphragm. This muscle is found at the bottom of the rib cage. The muscle contracts when a person breathes in. It moves down. This opens up space in

The diaphragm (modeled in red) separates the chest from the abdomen.

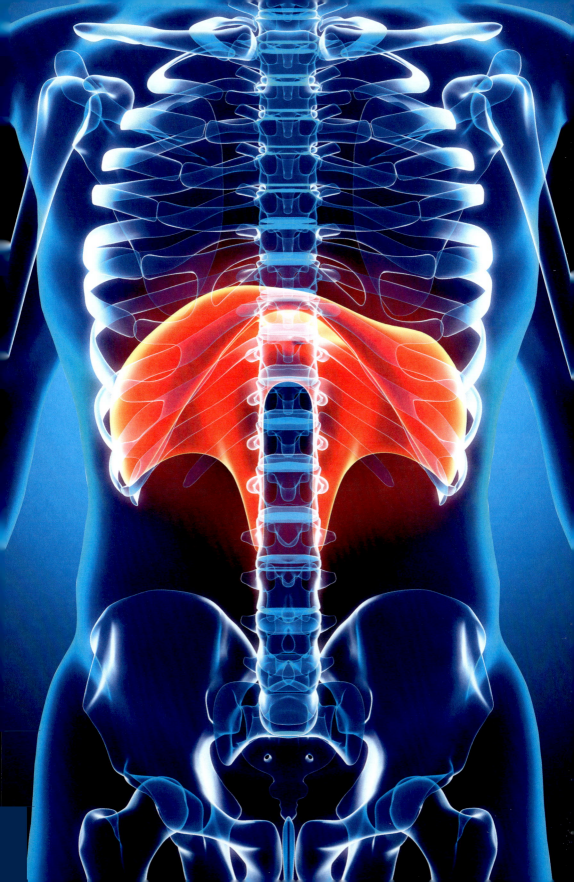

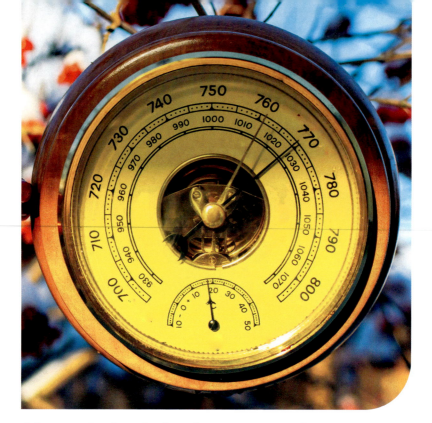

A barometer is a device that measures air pressure. The usual air pressure at sea level is 1,013.25 millibars (760 mm Hg).

the chest. Air moves inside the body to fill this space.

The diaphragm works by taking advantage of air pressure. The air on Earth is heavy. It presses down on the planet's surface. This causes air to rush into spaces of low pressure. The diaphragm makes such a space in the chest by increasing its volume. This reduces pressure. Air then rushes into the chest through the mouth and nose. The diaphragm moves up again when it relaxes. This raises the pressure within the chest. Gas within the body rushes out.

People do not usually have to think about using the diaphragm. It can contract on its own. This is because the brain sends automatic signals to the muscle. Biologist Gabrielle Kardon says, "We are completely dependent on the diaphragm. But we take it for granted every moment we're breathing."[3]

Inhaled air travels to the back of a person's throat. Air then moves into the trachea. This tube is sometimes called the windpipe. It marks the beginning of the lower airway.

THE HUMAN RESPIRATORY SYSTEM

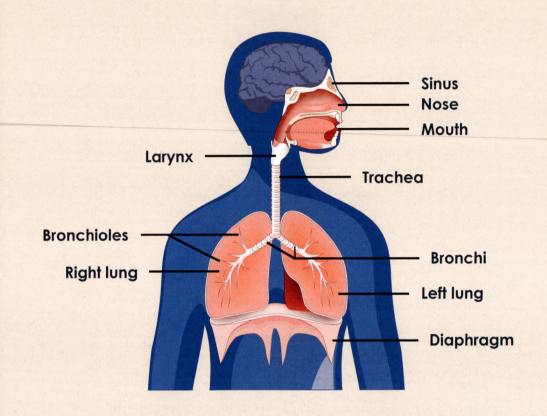

This diagram displays the parts of the upper and lower airways of the respiratory system.

The windpipe carries air to the bronchial tree. This is a network of airways. It is made up of bronchi and bronchioles. Bronchi carry air to the lungs. Bronchioles distribute air throughout the lungs. Air becomes warmer and moister in these airways. This makes exchanging gases in the blood easier.

THE LUNGS

The lungs are the largest organs of the respiratory system. A person normally has two lungs. They are located on each side of the heart. It is possible to live with only one lung.

Some people are born without two full lungs. Other people lose a lung due to injury or illness. People who have one lung can live normal lives. However, they may run out of breath faster than they would with two lungs. They may also experience some illnesses more severely than if they had two lungs.

Inside the lungs are tiny air sacs. They are called alveoli. Air meets red blood cells inside these sacs. These blood cells contain a protein called hemoglobin. This protein binds oxygen to the cells. The blood takes oxygen and leaves carbon dioxide. The blood then leaves the lungs to deliver oxygen throughout the body. Meanwhile, the carbon dioxide begins to leave the body. The gas escapes on the same route oxygen takes to enter the body.

A Small Difference in Size

The right lung is split up into three different sections called lobes. The left lung has only two lobes. This is because the heart rests in the space where the third lobe would be. This makes the left lung slightly smaller than the right lung.

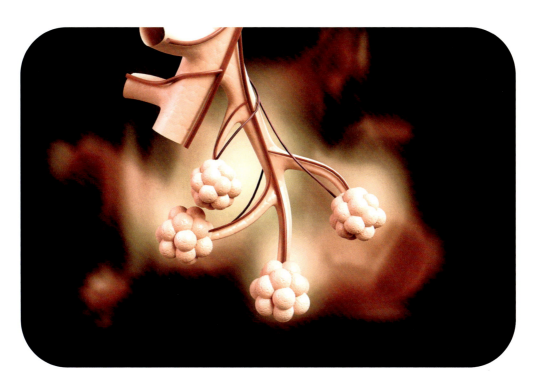

Alveoli form in groups called alveolar sacs. Each sac contains 20 to 30 alveoli.

The lungs contain hundreds of millions of alveoli. The alveoli increase the surface area of the lungs. This allows for more contact between the lungs and blood. Health writer Marjorie Hecht explains, "This large surface area is necessary to process the huge amounts of air involved in breathing."[4]

The lungs **inflate** during breathing. They deflate as waste gases leave the body.

Exhaled breath contains about 5 percent carbon dioxide. People also exhale oxygen that the body hasn't used. Finally, exhaled air contains nitrogen and other gases found in air.

There are eleven pairs of intercostal muscles located between the bones in the rib cage.

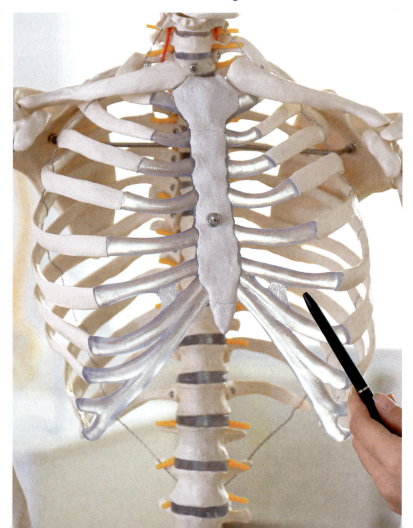

THE THORAX

The thorax protects the organs in a person's chest. These include the heart and lungs. The rib cage and spine support the thorax. Several muscles are also part of this structure.

The ribs play a big role in breathing. The intercostal muscles are located between a person's ribs. The intercostals contract and release much like the diaphragm. These muscles have three layers. The outer layer moves the ribs outward when a person breathes in. This increases space in the chest cavity. The two inner layers allow the ribs to move back inward when a person breathes out. This reduces space in the chest cavity.

CHAPTER THREE

WHAT CAN GO WRONG WITH THE RESPIRATORY SYSTEM?

Many illnesses and injuries affect the human respiratory system. Some respiratory conditions can harm a person's well-being. Serious conditions can even be fatal.

Asthma is one of the most common respiratory conditions. About 1 in 13 people in the United States suffers from it. Asthma can sometimes worsen quickly. The airways shrink. It becomes hard to breathe. This is

Doctors who work with the respiratory system are called pulmonologists.

Mild asthma attacks may last for only a few minutes. Severe attacks can last for hours or even days.

called an asthma attack. Many things can cause an asthma attack. These include exercise and allergies.

Doctors cannot cure asthma. But they can often treat it with inhalers. Some medicines relax the muscles in the airways. Others reduce **inflammation** in the lungs. These medicines can reduce the frequency and severity of asthma attacks.

RESPIRATORY VIRUSES

The common cold is a respiratory illness caused by **viruses**. There are more than 200 viruses that cause colds. Common signs of colds include a fever and a runny nose. People may also get a buildup of mucus. These symptoms are part of the body's response to the virus. They help the body kill the virus.

A cold is usually not a serious illness. Most people recover with little or no treatment. Some people are more likely to catch colds. They include children and people who smoke.

Influenza is another respiratory illness caused by viruses. Influenza is commonly called the flu. The flu can cause a stuffy nose, sore throat, and coughing. It can also cause inflammation in the lungs. Inflammation happens as the body tries to fight the virus. But too much inflammation can damage the lungs.

Cases of the flu range from mild to severe. Doctors recommend that people with the flu rest and drink enough water. Serious cases can be treated with medicine. The illness is most dangerous to young children and older people. The Centers

A stuffy nose happens when the lining of the nose becomes swollen due to inflammation.

for Disease Control and Prevention (CDC) reported that more than 44,900 Americans died from the flu during the 2023–2024 flu season.

COVID-19 is another respiratory disease caused by a virus. It began to spread across the world in 2020. This illness shares many mild symptoms with the flu. But COVID-19 is more likely than the flu to become severe. Some COVID-19 patients develop dangerous conditions such as pneumonia. Pneumonia is inflammation of the lungs. The CDC reported that almost 1.2 million Americans died from COVID-19 between January 1, 2020, and August 10, 2024. People with asthma and other respiratory illnesses face greater risks of severe illness from COVID-19.

People can take vaccines for the flu and COVID-19. Vaccines are substances designed to help people resist infectious diseases. They usually contain weakened versions of the infectious germ. Vaccines are typically injected into people. They can also be sprayed into the nose. The body then becomes familiar with the germ.

Ventilators

Ventilators are machines that breathe for people. They are used when people cannot breathe on their own. Serious illnesses can shut down the respiratory system. Ventilators can help people survive while doctors treat illnesses. People must also be placed on ventilators when they have certain types of surgeries. This helps them get enough oxygen during the procedures.

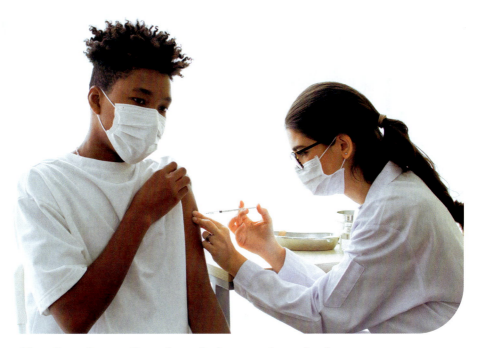

Vaccines have played a role in greatly reducing or even eliminating certain serious diseases, such as polio and smallpox.

This allows the body to fight it much better than it could before. Vaccines for respiratory viruses can reduce the spread of diseases. They can also reduce the severity of illnesses.

COPD AND LUNG CANCER

Chronic obstructive **pulmonary** disease (COPD) is a serious lung condition. It

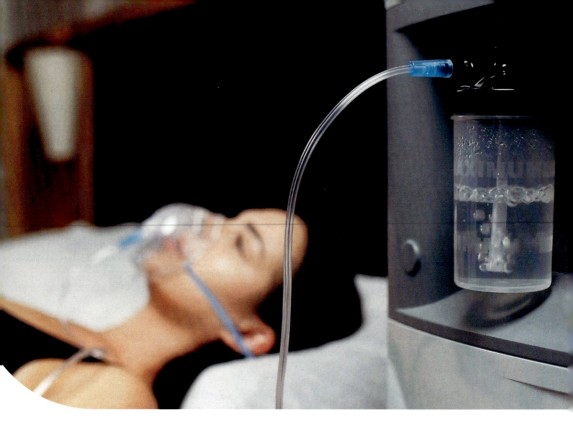

An oxygen concentrator is a device sometimes used by people with COPD. This device increases the amount of oxygen in the air that a person breathes.

makes it hard for people to get enough oxygen into their lungs. The most common cause of COPD is smoking tobacco. Smoking damages the airways and lungs. This damage can make it hard for people to breathe. COPD causes the lungs to lose their stretchy quality. They overexpand when they take in air. They then have trouble moving all the air out. Some of it gets trapped inside the body. This can be uncomfortable and sometimes dangerous.

Meredith Lores suffers from COPD. Health workers help her control her symptoms. She uses an inhaler. She eats healthy food. And she goes for regular walks. Healthy breathing practices help as well. But sometimes her COPD flares up. She went to the hospital for it in 2017. "I wasn't in control of my breathing and it was terrifying," she remembers.[5]

Rodney has had COPD for more than 20 years. One of his first signs was shortness of breath. He felt this when carrying his 5-year-old son. He does a lot to control his COPD. This includes not smoking. He says, "Quitting smoking was the best thing I could have done. . . . It gave me a more confident and grateful attitude."[6]

Another serious respiratory illness is lung cancer. Like COPD, lung cancer is often caused by smoking. Tobacco smoke contains at least seventy **carcinogens**. Lung cancer can cause growths called tumors. Tumors can put pressure on the lungs. This can make breathing difficult. Tumors can also cause inflammation. Large tumors can even block a patient's airways. Lung cancer can also spread to other parts of the body.

It is possible to get lung cancer without ever smoking tobacco. Between 10 and 20 percent of people with the disease have never smoked. This form of the illness is more common in women. It also tends to

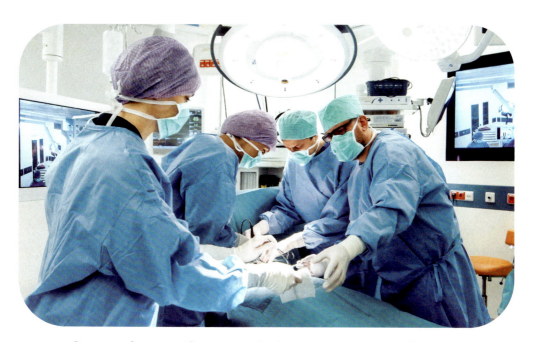

Surgery is sometimes needed to remove tumors from a patient's lungs.

strike nonsmokers younger than those who have a history of smoking. Lung cancer has a high **mortality** rate. Only about 19 percent of people diagnosed with the disease live 5 years or longer.

WHEN PEOPLE CANNOT GET ENOUGH AIR

Suffocation occurs when the body cannot get enough air. Without oxygen, brain damage and even death can occur within minutes. Many situations can cause suffocation. One of these situations is choking. Food is among the most common substances that get stuck in the windpipe. The bottom of the throat has two passages.

The Heimlich maneuver is one way to treat choking. People can learn how to use the Heimlich maneuver by taking first aid classes.

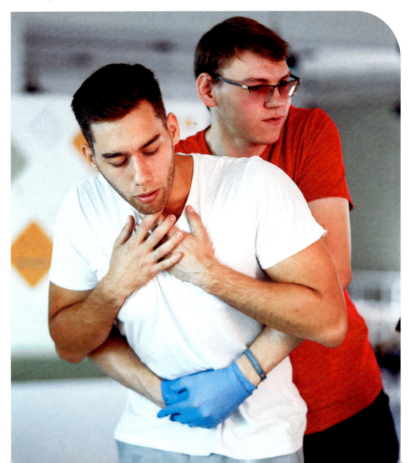

The first is the esophagus. This tube carries food to the stomach. The other passage is the windpipe. Food that enters the windpipe can block air from reaching the lungs.

Drowning is another situation that causes suffocation. Most people can hold their breath underwater for between 30 seconds and 2 minutes. Eventually, the body forces itself to breathe. Water that enters the windpipe travels to the lungs. This prevents a drowning person from getting air. Many drowning accidents happen in pools, lakes, and oceans. But drowning can also happen in bathtubs and other shallow water.

CHAPTER FOUR

WHAT CAN HUMANS DO TO KEEP THE RESPIRATORY SYSTEM HEALTHY?

People with healthy respiratory systems are less likely to suffer from certain illnesses. Sometimes air contains unwanted materials. Healthy lungs can help keep inhaled germs and **pollutants** from making people sick. Special cells in the alveoli destroy these invaders. This helps prevent infections.

Avoiding smoking helps keep the respiratory system healthy. Over time,

Air contains countless germs, but the body is good at filtering out dangerous invaders.

According to the CDC, cigarette smoking kills more than 480,000 people in the United States each year.

smoking narrows a person's airways. It also stiffens the airways. These changes make it harder for the lungs to do their job. Vaping also has many harmful effects on the lungs.

Smoking increases a person's chance of illnesses such as COPD and lung cancer. It has also been linked to many other types of cancer. It raises the risk of cancer in the mouth, nose, and throat. Smoking even raises the risk of cancer forming in body parts outside the respiratory system.

SECONDHAND SMOKE

People who choose not to smoke do not improve only their own health. They also improve the health of those around them. Secondhand smoke is released from burning cigarettes. It is also exhaled by smokers. Secondhand smoke can cause many of the same illnesses as direct smoke. Secondhand smoke can also irritate the eyes and airways of nonsmokers. Children who breathe secondhand smoke are more likely to develop asthma. They are also more likely to suffer from ear infections.

Many places in the United States are smoke-free by law. This helps protect

Many states have laws banning smoking in places such as restaurants, workplaces, and government buildings.

people from exposure to secondhand smoke. Dr. Corinne Graffunder is the director of the CDC's Office on Smoking and Health. She states, "We know what works to reduce secondhand smoke exposure. Smoke-free environments are the best way to fully protect all people from the dangers of secondhand smoke."[7]

AVOIDING OTHER POLLUTANTS

According to the World Health Organization (WHO), 99 percent of people are exposed to polluted air. Vehicles and other sources of pollution release harmful substances into the air. Even natural disasters such as forest fires can pollute the air.

Many types of air pollution come in the form of particulate matter (PM). People can easily inhale PM. Common PM includes dust and smoke. Some PM is so small that it cannot be seen with the naked eye. All PM can cause health problems. But the smallest PM is the most dangerous. This is because these particles travel deep into the respiratory system.

Open fires are used for cooking in many parts of the world. They are another source of air pollution. Dr. Tedros Adhanom Ghebreyesus is the director-general of WHO. He says, "Air pollution threatens us all, but the poorest and most **marginalized** people bear the brunt of the burden."[8] He explains that more than 3 billion people inhale air pollution from unhealthy stoves and fuels used at home.

If worn properly, some masks can filter out almost all particulate matter.

There are ways people can reduce the amount of PM they breathe. One is by staying indoors when air quality is poor. Many buildings have systems that filter the air. People can also wear masks that filter inhaled air.

EATING HEALTHY AND EXERCISING

Eating a healthy diet can help keep the respiratory system working properly. Vitamins and minerals protect the lungs from stress and inflammation. Unhealthy foods can have the opposite effect.

Keeping one's weight within a healthy range also helps the respiratory system stay in good shape. Excess weight in the abdomen makes it harder for the diaphragm to expand the lungs. This results in less oxygen moving into the body.

Regular exercise is a big part of overall health. But it can be especially important for the respiratory system. Exercise improves lung function. It also makes the body better at drawing oxygen into the blood. This helps people breathe better when exercising. People can then exercise for longer. This creates a healthy cycle for the respiratory system.

Reducing the Chance of Illness

The CDC says that regular handwashing can prevent about 20 percent of respiratory infections. The CDC also recommends avoiding contact with those who are sick with a contagious illness. This is another way to reduce the chances of getting ill.

In the United States, packaged food is labeled with the ingredients and nutrients it contains.

The US government has guidelines on healthy physical activity. These guidelines say that people should get at least 150 minutes of moderate exercise per week. This kind of exercise includes walking fast or pushing a lawnmower. The guidelines say people can also choose to do at least 75 minutes of vigorous exercise. This includes running or swimming laps.

Jumping rope is an example of a vigorous exercise.

Following these guidelines can improve respiratory health.

The human body is an amazing thing. Each system plays a big role in keeping the body alive. This includes the respiratory system. Every cell in the human body needs oxygen. This makes it especially important that people take care of their respiratory system.

GLOSSARY

carcinogens

substances that cause cancer

inflammation

redness, swelling, pain, or heat around a body part that is healing or removing an outside invader

inflate

to increase in size by taking in air

marginalized

treated as unimportant

mortality

death

pollutants

substances that contaminate the environment

pulmonary

relating to the lungs

sinuses

hollow spaces in the skull surrounding the nose

viruses

infectious agents that often spread rapidly and cause disease

SOURCE NOTES

INTRODUCTION: HELPING PEOPLE BREATHE

1. Quoted in "'Correct Technique of Using an Inhaler Is So Important' | Professor Su May Liew, 48," *The University of Edinburgh*, June 13, 2024. www.ed.ac.uk.

CHAPTER ONE: WHAT IS THE RESPIRATORY SYSTEM?

2. Dr. Shawn Nishi, "Breathe Easy: Keeping Our Lungs Healthy," *UTMB Health*, October 14, 2021. www.utmb.edu.

CHAPTER TWO: HOW DOES THE RESPIRATORY SYSTEM WORK?

3. Quoted in Carl Zimmer, "Behind Each Breath, an Underappreciated Muscle," *New York Times*, April 2, 2015. www.nytimes.com.

4. Marjorie Hecht, "The Alveoli in Your Lungs," *Healthline*, July 18, 2024. www.healthline.com.

CHAPTER THREE: WHAT CAN GO WRONG WITH THE RESPIRATORY SYSTEM?

5. Quoted in "Meredith's Story," *Lung Foundation Australia*, n.d. https://lungfoundation.com.au.

6. Quoted in "Life with COPD: Patient Shares His Story of Positivity and Perseverance," *AstraZeneca*, July 24, 2020. www.astrazeneca-us.com.

CHAPTER FOUR: WHAT CAN HUMANS DO TO KEEP THE RESPIRATORY SYSTEM HEALTHY?

7. Quoted in Dr. Sumir Shah, "Secondhand Smoke Still a Problem for Americans: CDC," *ABC News*, December 6, 2018. https://abcnews.go.com.

8. Quoted in "9 out of 10 People Worldwide Breathe Polluted Air, but More Countries Are Taking Action," *World Health Organization*, May 2, 2018. www.who.int.

FOR FURTHER RESEARCH

BOOKS

Cassie M. Lawton, *The Human Respiratory System*. New York: Cavendish Square, 2021.

Leigh McClure, *The Respiratory System*. Buffalo, NY: Scientific American Educational Publishing, 2025.

Chelsea Xie, *The Circulatory System*. San Diego, CA: BrightPoint Press, 2025.

INTERNET SOURCES

"How Lungs Work," *American Lung Association*, September 29, 2023. www.lung.org.

"The Process of Breathing," *BBC*, n.d. www.bbc.co.uk.

"Smoking and Physical Activity," *Cleveland Clinic*, July 27, 2021. https://my.clevelandclinic.org.

WEBSITES

American Lung Association
www.lung.org

The American Lung Association's website provides a variety of health information about the respiratory system. This includes information about respiratory diseases, air pollution, and the health effects of smoking.

MedlinePlus
www.medlineplus.gov

MedlinePlus is an official website of the US government. It provides information on a range of health topics, including the respiratory system.

The Real Cost
https://therealcost.betobaccofree.hhs.gov

The Real Cost is a health campaign run by the US government. Its website gives people information about the health effects of tobacco use and vaping.

INDEX

alveoli, 28–29, 46
asthma, 6–10, 32–34, 37, 49

blood, 11, 15–17, 20, 27–29, 54
bronchi, 26
bronchioles, 26

carbon dioxide, 16–17, 28, 30
cells, 15–16, 18, 28, 46, 57
chronic obstructive pulmonary disease (COPD), 39–42, 48
cilia, 20
common cold, 35
COVID-19, 37–38

diaphragm, 22–26, 31, 53–54

eating well, 53
exercising, 17, 34, 54–57

heart, 15–16, 27–28, 31
hemoglobin, 28

influenza, 35–38
inhalers, 9, 34, 41
intercostal muscles, 31

larynx, 18, 26
Liew, Su May, 6–10
lung cancer, 42–43, 48–49
lungs, 9, 26–31, 34, 36–37, 39–43, 45, 46–48, 53–54

mucus, 21, 35

nostrils, 20

oxygen, 11, 12–17, 28, 30, 38, 40, 43–44, 54, 57

particulate matter (PM), 51–53

secondhand smoke, 49–50
sinuses, 22, 26
smelling, 11, 18
smoking, 35, 40–43, 46–50
suffocation, 43–45

thorax, 31
trachea, 25–26, 44–45

vaccines, 38–39
ventilators, 38
vocal cords, 18–19

yawning, 17

IMAGE CREDITS

Cover: © Esther Pueyo/Shutterstock Images
5: © illustrissima/Shutterstock Images
7: © Thicha Satapitanon/Shutterstock Images
8: © Africa Studio/Shutterstock Images
10: © Helena Nechaeva/Shutterstock Images
13: © PeopleImages.com-Yuri A./Shutterstock Images
14: © Pixel-Shot/Shutterstock Images
16: © Elnur/Shutterstock Images
19: © Monkey Business Images/Shutterstock Images
20: © Krakenimages.com/Shutterstock Images
23: © MDGRPHCS/Shutterstock Images
24: © Petr Merkurev/Shutterstock Images
26: © Designua/Shutterstock Images
29: © Liya Graphics/Shutterstock Images
30: © New Africa/Shutterstock Images
33: © Dragon Images/Shutterstock Images
34: © Pixel-Shot/Shutterstock Images
36: © Prostock-Studio/Shutterstock Images
39: © Ann Rodchua/Shutterstock Images
40: © wedmoments.stock/Shutterstock Images
43: © Gorodenkoff/Shutterstock Images
44: © UfaBizPhoto/Shutterstock Images
47: © nikkimeel/Shutterstock Images
48: © leolintang/Shutterstock Images
50: © PoohFotoz/Shutterstock Images
52: © SvedOliver/Shutterstock Images
55: © Billy F. Blume Jr./Shutterstock Images
56: © Ground Picture/Shutterstock Images

ABOUT THE AUTHOR

Tammy Gagne is an author and editor who specializes in nonfiction. She has written hundreds of books for both young people and adults. She lives in northern New England with her husband, son, and dogs.